Life as a New Mom
(The real truths)

ISBN-13:
978-1985387201

ISBN-10:
1985387204

M3 Publishing, Embrun, ON, Canada

Life as a New Mom

(The real truths)

Congratulations, you are a new mom or about to be one! This will be one of the most exciting and exhausting times of your life.

This book is intended to inform you of the amusing and peculiar things people usually don't tell you about being a new mom.

HORMONES

Your body has been on overdrive with hormones for the last 9 months and now that baby is born, these hormones don't just disappear.

You may experience tears of joy & sadness
all in one cry.

You may feel frustrated.....with everything.

You just may forget your baby at home.

You may experience post partum
depression.
(This is more common than people realize).

You may feel overwhelmed with a new baby
at home.

You may not know how to use a car seat or
any other baby gadget.

You may feel like you aren't good enough.

You may feel like you don't know what you
are doing.

Babies don't come with instructions;
unfortunately.

A child can never have enough love.

You may actually appreciate your own mom
a little more (tell her so).

Late night feedings are exhausting.

The house does not have to be in perfect order; you have a new baby at home who needs your attention.

You will feel sleep deprived.
Oh wait, you likely are!

<u>BOOBIES</u>

21

They will hurt.

They will fill with milk.

Your boobies will leak; at some points,
large amounts.

Nursing pads (even if you are not nursing)
are a life saver.

Try to avoid white tops....
Image when your boobies leak.

You may need to use a heat lamp on your boobies for breast feeding. You feel like a piece of meat in a grocery store under the heat light. Not fun.

You can pump milk (with a machine or your hands) to release pressure from your boobies.

Your boobies will likely release milk or 'leak'
when you hear a baby cry; any baby.

You may not want your partner to touch
'the gals' as they will be sensitive.

Some partners want to taste breast milk;
right from the source.

You may have had a tear. OUCH!

You may have been cut, so you didn't tear.
OUCH!

You may have stitches 'down there'.
Don't worry, they will be dissolvable.

You may need to take a sitz bath if you were cut or tore to help you heal. This is where you place a bowl (usually given by the hospital) in the toilet hole with warm water and usually Epsom salts.

Some hospitals will give you a bottle to
hose yourself instead of the sitz bath. It
does not hurt, although it does feel
worrisome at first.

The very first poop after your baby will
likely feel scary. You may think it will hurt, it
usually does not.

For most women after a baby, the thought of having sex is the last thing on their mind. You can always use the "I have to wait for my 6 week check up" reason to hold out for now.

FAMILY & FRIENDS

Your family and friends will be so happy for you.

Some family or friends may feel slightly
jealous if they are trying to conceive.

People will constantly be throwing their
advice at you. They mean well.

People will be telling you *their* baby stories.

Do what you feel is right for you and your
baby.

Allow yourself time to heal;
you had major surgery.

You may not be able to pick up your baby
right away. This can be quite emotional.

Get plenty of rest.

Allow others to help you.

Cuddle with your baby.

<u>BABY TIME</u>

Babies are a lot of work, but they are so
worth it.

Your baby will grow up right before your
eyes; enjoy every moment.

Babies like to eat, all the time.

Try to sleep when your baby sleeps.
The housework can wait.

Your partner may not be able to get up with baby for night time feedings if he/she is working.

For the first few weeks, you will notice your
baby has a cycle.
EAT – SLEEP – PEE/POOP
Then repeat.

Allow your partner to participate in baby's care.

Enjoy bath time with your baby.

Pets may feel jealous of baby and react
(Example: peeing in baby's bed or hiding
baby's toys).

Your partner may feel neglected with your
attention focused on baby.

Melanie McCully lives in Ontario and has a passion for writing. Melanie has written several other books, as mentioned below.

"Diary of a Surrogate" is Melanie's own personal journey of becoming a surrogate mother.

"What you need to know if you can't get pregnant ~Within Canada" is just what the title states. Topics include but not limited to, the law, psychology, religion, possible medical causes and treatments, donors, adoption and support groups.

"I Love You gros gros comme le ciel" is a children's book about a mother's love.

"Dear Self" is a book of quotes that Melanie has learned over the years; some of them the hard way.